Marriage
JOURNAL

Thirty-One Days With God and My Marriage

by

Jeff Hendley

Library of Congress
Control Number: 2005900528

ISBN: 0-9762014-2-9

Published by L'Edge Press
A division of Upside Down Ministries, Inc.
Boone, North Carolina

Translations

I have chosen to use various translations and paraphrases to help in the reading and understanding of these passages. If you have a favorite translation, then just turn to the passage in your Bible and read it from that translation.

The Old Testament was written in Hebrew and the New Testament was written in Greek. In fact, the Greek language of the New Testament was the "market" language of that time. This means it was the street language or the everyday language that the people used to speak to one another.

Therefore, it helps us to understand what the Bible is saying when we take the original Hebrew and Greek and translate it into our everyday language that we use to communicate. These various translations in this journal are a reflection of the translations that have been done over the past decades.

Dedication

This journal is dedicated to all those who desire to have a marriage that is exceptional. By this I mean exceptionally healthy, exceptionally mature, exceptional by the standards of the world and excepts nothing but the best for each person in the marriage.

As we begin, let these words of Jesus in *The Message* ignite our hearts:

> *One day the Pharisees were badgering him: 'Is it legal for a man to divorce his wife for any reason?' He answered, 'Haven't you read in your Bible that the Creator originally made man and woman for each other, male and female? And because of this, a man leaves father and mother and is firmly bonded to his wife, becoming one flesh—no longer two bodies but one. Because God created this organic union of the two sexes, no one should desecrate his art by cutting them apart.'*

> *They shot back in rebuttal, 'If that's so why did Moses give instructions for divorce papers and divorce procedures?'*

> *Jesus said, 'Moses provided for divorce as a concession to your hardheartedness, but it is not part of God's original plan. I'm holding you to the original plan, and holding you liable for adultery if you divorce your faithful wife and then marry someone else. I make an exception in cases where the spouse has committed adultery.'*

> *Jesus' disciples objected, 'If those are the terms of marriage, we're stuck. Why get married?'*

> *But Jesus said, 'Not everyone is mature enough to live a married life. It requires a certain aptitude and grace. Marriage isn't for everyone. Some, from birth seemingly, never give marriage a thought. Others never get asked— or accepted. And some decide not to get married for kingdom reasons. But if you're capable of growing into the largeness of marriage, do it.'*

The Message, Matthew 19:3-12

Introduction

In *Upside Down Marriage*, the first marriage is scripted:

"In the beginning, God's creative juices were flowing. Light. Dark. Water. Land. Oceans. Animals. Man. Fish. Plants. After each major creative event, God looked over all He had done and declared that it was "good." This declaration occurred six times in a row. Six times God declared, "It is good" about what He had created.

But then there was a bump in the road. He looked at man and it occurred to God that something was not good. God looked and said that it was not good for man to be alone. God saw a great need in His creation. Something that was not good needed to be made good. He wanted all of His creation to be good, complete and full. He began to search for what would complete the goodness of His creation.

Nothing God had created to this point satisfied this goodness. Adam reviewed all of the animals God created and even named them. This was not the answer to the missing goodness. God put His creativity to work again. He put Adam to sleep and took a part of Adam and created "woman." God brought her to him.

When Adam opened his eyes—he knew. He knew that God had taken a part of him and created his counter-part. He gazed upon the first "woman" and she gazed upon him. They both knew that they were a part of each other and were meant for each other. They both knew that this was the answer to God's search to fill the goodness need in His creation. Woman and man...part of each other. Linked. Inseparable. Together God placed them in the Garden to rule over His creation. God stepped back and looked. He saw everything He had created. Down through the heavens and down through the ages His resounding voice can be heard, "It is very good...""

God wants happiness in marriage. He wants cheerfulness in our homes. He wants the wife to be happy. He knows this can be accomplished when the husband takes it upon himself. God has given this "quest" to each husband. It becomes our calling not for one year only but for our entire lives. Our crusade, our quest, our adventure as husbands is to fight, battle, and insure that we bring happiness to our wives. We are to make it possible for them to have a happy home. We are to bring happiness and cheer into their lives. Nothing can stand in our way or deter us from our task.

(*Upside Down Marriage*, 50-51)

Dr. James Dobson, President of Focus on the Family, gives a stirring image of what he thinks women need. Even though this was written three decades ago, these thoughts are still relevant for today:

Joyce Landorf, the gifted authoress of *His Stubborn Love*, recently asked people to answer the following question: What would you change about women in general if you could wave some sort of magic wand? My answer, which is now published with the other replies in her book *The Fragrance of Beauty*, is quoted below:

If I could write a prescription for women of the world, I would provide each one of them with a healthy dose of self-esteem and personal worth (taken three times a day until the symptoms disappear). I have no doubt that this is their greatest need...If women felt genuinely respected in their role as wives and mothers, they would not need to abandon it for something better. If they felt equal with men in personal worth, they would not need to be equivalent to men in responsibility. If they could bask in the dignity and status granted them by the Creator, then their femininity would be valued as their greatest asset, rather than scorned as an old garment to be discarded. Without question, the future of a nation depends on how it sees its women, and I hope we will teach our little girls to be glad they were chosen by God for the special pleasure of womanhood. (Dobson, 35)

These are two examples of how the pen can put our thoughts on paper. This journal is for marriages. Marriages yet to be and marriages that already are.

The instructions are simple.

1) **Read a passage each day.** If you skip a day or two just record the current date on the date line and keep on going. There is no pressure to read this every day.

2) **Think about what you have just read.** What do these words have to say to you and your marriage? Watch this one. The question is not what do these words have to say to your spouse. But what the words are saying to you.

3) **Talk/Pray.** Have a conversation with God about these words. They are His words and He knows why He wrote them. Ask Him questions and discuss what it means for you in your marriage.

4) **Dream.** Ephesians 3:20 says, "Now to him who is able to do immeasurably more than all we ask or imagine, according to his power that is at work in us..."(NIV) Dream about what kind of marriage you want to have. Dream about what you can do to improve your marriage and love your spouse better.

5) **Write down your thoughts.** For one month keep track of what is on your mind and what is on your heart. It may surprise you when you go back later and read what you have written down. Who knows—maybe you will end up with a poem, a song, or even a book.

6) **Talk with each other.** Discuss what you have read and written in your journal.

Enjoy this time thinking through your marriage and having a discussion with God. Use this time to allow God to renew your heart and to refresh you and your marriage.

Marriage Journal

Name   _____

Spouse's Name _____

Wedding Date _____

Genesis 1:26-31

[26]God spoke: "Let us make human beings in our image, make them reflecting our nature
So they can be responsible for the fish in the sea,
the birds in the air, the cattle,
And, yes, Earth itself,
and every animal that moves on the face of Earth."
[27]God created human beings;
he created them godlike,
Reflecting God's nature.
He created them male and female.
[28]God blessed them:
"Prosper! Reproduce! Fill Earth! Take charge!
Be responsible for fish in the sea and birds in the air,
for every living thing that moves on the face of Earth."

[29]Then God said, "I've given you
every sort of seed-bearing plant on Earth
And every kind of fruit-bearing tree,
given them to you for food.
[30]To all animals and all birds,
everything that moves and breathes,
I give whatever grows out of the ground for food."
And there it was.

[31]God looked over everything he had made;
it was so good, so very good!
It was evening, it was morning--
Day Six.   MSG

"Everyman dies. But not everyman lives."
(*Braveheart*)

Genesis 2:18-25

[18]Now the Lord God said, It is not good (sufficient, satisfactory) that the man should be alone; I will make him a helper meet (suitable, adapted, complementary) for him.

[19]And out of the ground the Lord God formed every [wild] beast and living creature of the field and every bird of the air and brought them to Adam to see what he would call them; and whatever Adam called every living creature, that was its name.

[20]And Adam gave names to all the livestock and to the birds of the air and to every [wild] beast of the field; but for Adam there was not found a helper meet (suitable, adapted, complementary) for him.

[21]And the Lord God caused a deep sleep to fall upon Adam; and while he slept, He took one of his ribs or a part of his side and closed up the [place with] flesh.

[22]And the rib or part of his side which the Lord God had taken from the man He built up and made into a woman, and He brought her to the man.

[23]Then Adam said, This [creature] is now bone of my bones and flesh of my flesh; she shall be called Woman, because she was taken out of a man.

[24]Therefore a man shall leave his father and his mother and shall become united and cleave to his wife, and they shall become one flesh.

[25]And the man and his wife were both naked and were not embarrassed or ashamed in each other's presence.   AMP

In *Apples of Gold* (a collection of sayings and quotes) the following quote illustrates God's creation of woman:

> Creation of woman from the rib of man:
> she was not made of his head to top him;
> nor out of his feet to be trampled upon by him;
> but out of his side to be equal to him;
> under his arm to be protected;
> and near his heart to be beloved.

Day 3

Deuteronomy 24:5

5 When a man has taken a new wife, he shall not go out to war or be charged with any business; he shall be free at home one year, and bring happiness to his wife whom he has taken. NKJV

_____

_____

_____

_____

_____

_____

_____

_____

_____

_____

_____

_____

_____

_____

_____

_____

_____

_____

_____

_____

Day 4   Date: _____

Psalm 127:1-2
¹Unless the LORD builds the house,
  those who build it labor in vain.
Unless the LORD watches over the city,
  the watchman stays awake in vain.
²It is in vain that you rise up early
  and go late to rest,
eating the bread of anxious toil;
  for he gives to his beloved sleep. ESV

_____
_____
_____
_____
_____
_____
_____
_____
_____
_____
_____
_____
_____
_____
_____
_____

Day 5

Proverbs 5:15-23

[15]Drink waters out of your own cistern [of a pure marriage relationship], and fresh running waters out of your own well.

[16]Should your offspring be dispersed abroad as water brooks in the streets? [17][Confine yourself to your own wife] let your children be for you alone, and not the children of strangers with you.

[18]Let your fountain [of human life] be blessed [with the rewards of fidelity], and rejoice in the wife of your youth.

[19]Let her be as the loving hind and pleasant doe [tender, gentle, attractive]-- let her bosom satisfy you at all times, and always be transported with delight in her love.

[20]Why should you, my son, be infatuated with a loose woman, embrace the bosom of an outsider, and go astray?

[21]For the ways of man are directly before the eyes of the Lord, and He [Who would have us live soberly, chastely, and godly] carefully weighs all man's goings.

[22]His own iniquities shall ensnare the wicked man, and he shall be held with the cords of his sin.

[23]He will die for lack of discipline and instruction, and in the greatness of his folly he will go astray and be lost.   AMP

All The Way

Somewhere I read, dear Lord
That You want us to have the most
Out of our physical intimacy—
Not the least…
That You want to bring
Into our sexual experience
An overwhelming spirit of sensitivity…
That You are eager for us
To celebrate our consuming love
In a pleasurable, exciting way…
That within our marriage relationship
You have ordained sex to be
An indescribable experience
A fantastic adventure
A rich fulfillment…

That You delight for us to share
Freely, generously, totally
In the most profound
Of all human relationships…
That you never intended our oneness
To be less than the best
Lord, we're with You all the way!
Thank You!   (Calkin, 25)

Matthew 5:21-24

[21]"You have heard that the law of Moses says, `Do not murder. If you commit murder, you are subject to judgment.' [22]But I say, if you are angry with someone, you are subject to judgment! If you call someone an idiot, you are in danger of being brought before the high council. And if you curse someone, you are in danger of the fires of hell."

[23]"So if you are standing before the altar in the Temple, offering a sacrifice to God, and you suddenly remember that someone has something against you, [24]leave your sacrifice there beside the altar. Go and be reconciled to that person. Then come and offer your sacrifice to God." NLT

Yet it is in this whole process of meeting and solving problems that our life has its meaning. Problems are the cutting edge that distinguishes between success and failure. Problems call forth our courage and our wisdom; indeed, they create our courage and wisdom. It is only because of problems that we grow mentally and spiritually. When we desire to encourage the growth of the human spirit, we challenge and encourage the human capacity to solve problems, just as in school we deliberately set problems for our children to solve. It is through the pain of confronting and resolving problems that we learn. As Benjamin Franklin said, "Those things that hurt, instruct." It is for this reason that wise people learn not to dread but actually to welcome problems and actually to welcome the pain of problems.

Most of us are not so wise. Fearing the pain involved, almost all of us, to a greater or lesser degree, attempt to avoid problems. We procrastinate, hoping that they will go away. We ignore them, forget them, pretend they do not exist. We even take drugs to assist us in ignoring them, so that by deadening ourselves to the pain we can forget the problems that cause the pain. We attempt to skirt around problems rather than meet them head on. We attempt to get out of them rather than suffer through them. (Peck, 16)

Matthew 7:1-5

[1]Don't pick on people, jump on their failures, criticize their faults--unless, of course, you want the same treatment. [2]That critical spirit has a way of boomeranging. [3]It's easy to see a smudge on your neighbor's face and be oblivious to the ugly sneer on your own. [4]Do you have the nerve to say, "Let me wash your face for you,' when your own face is distorted by contempt? [5]It's this whole traveling road-show mentality all over again, playing a holier-than-thou part instead of just living your part. Wipe that ugly sneer off your own face, and you might be fit to offer a washcloth to your neighbor. MSG

Matthew 7:1-5

[1] "Do not judge so that you will not be judged.
[2] "For in the way you judge, you will be judged; and by your standard of measure, it will be measured to you.
[3] "Why do you look at the speck that is in your brother's eye, but do not notice the log that is in your own eye?
[4] " Or how can you say to your brother, 'Let me take the speck out of your eye,' and behold, the log is in your own eye?
[5] "You hypocrite, first take the log out of your own eye, and then you will see clearly to take the speck out of your brother's eye." NASB

"I got gaps, she's got gaps. Together we fill gaps."
(Rocky Balboa, *Rocky 1*)

Proverbs 27:17

[17] As iron sharpens iron,
so one man sharpens another. NIV

Shining Reward

O dear Lord
How unprepared we were
For the breathtaking surprises
Awaiting us in our marriage.
We simply didn't know
How much we didn't know.
We couldn't see
Every part of marriage.
But we knew we had promised
What we couldn't see.
It didn't take long to discover
That marriage wasn't the end of struggle.
All of a sudden it was just the beginning.
But the one shining reward
Through the fleeting years is this:
While we've shared the struggles
We've doubled the joys!   (Calkin, 24)

Matthew 7:7-12

[7]Ask and it will be given to you; seek and you will find; knock and the door will be opened to you. [8]For everyone who asks receives; he who seeks finds; and to him who knocks, the door will be opened.
[9]Which of you, if his son asks for bread, will give him a stone? [10]Or if he asks for a fish, will give him a snake? [11]If you, then, though you are evil, know how to give good gifts to your children, how much more will your Father in heaven give good gifts to those who ask him! [12]So in everything, do to others what you would have them do to you, for this sums up the Law and the Prophets. NIV

Marriage

Marriage!
It's rough. It's tough. It's work.
Anybody who says it isn't
Has never been married.
Marriage has far bigger problems
Than toothpaste squeezed
From the middle of the tube.

Marriage means...
Grappling, aching, struggling.
It means putting up
With personality weaknesses
Accepting criticism
And giving each other freedom to fail.
It means sharing deep feelings
About fear and rejection.
It means turning self-pity into laughter
And taking a walk to gain control.

Marriage means...
Gentleness and joy
Toughness and fortitude
Fairness and forgiveness
And a walloping amount of sacrifice.

Marriage means...
Learning when to say nothing
When to keep talking
When to push a little
When to back off.
It means acknowledging
"I can't be God to you—
I need Him, too."

Marriage means...
You are the other part of me
I am the other part of you.
We'll work through
With never a thought of walking out.

Marriage means...
Two imperfect mates
Building permanently
Giving totally
In partnership with a perfect God.
Marriage, my love, means us!

(Calkin, 43)

Matthew 20:25-28

[25]But Jesus called them together and said, "You know that in this world kings are tyrants, and officials lord it over the people beneath them. [26]But among you it should be quite different. Whoever wants to be a leader among you must be your servant, [27]and whoever wants to be first must become your slave. [28]For even I, the Son of Man, came here not to be served but to serve others, and to give my life as a ransom for many." ESV

We have to decide whether or not we are going to be spectators or players. Watching a basketball game is fun. Attending a pep rally for our favorite team is exciting. Having season tickets is nice. But this is one game we do not want to be sitting in the stands watching others play. We do not want to be on the sidelines cheering for our teams or for our families. We want to come away from this one game, this one adventure with sweat on our brows, dirt on our pants, soreness in our muscles, and hearts filled with excitement. We do not want to be left behind while other couples move ahead in their marriages.

Marriage is the adventure of a lifetime. The game of all games. The sport of all sports. A healthy marriage, a healthy home is worth the price. It is worth the hard work. It is worth the sweat equity. It is one time when we should not mind getting banged up and bruised. It is one game for which we do not want to miss the practices that lead up to the game. We will become better husbands due to the hard work and the practicing.

All husbands need to be around other men who are playing and coaching in this kind of game. We need to be with men who are committed to this game and who want it bad. We need to be with men who are playing in or have played in the game of marriage. We need men who have become bruised, dirty and sweaty while taking on the issues of marriage. Gentlemen, we need to be meeting over coffee, for breakfast, or at seminars. We need to get together in order to encourage each other to work hard, love hard, and build healthy homes. (*Upside Down Marriage*, 34-35)

Day 11

Matthew 22:37-40

[37]Jesus replied: " 'Love the Lord your God with all your heart and with all your soul and with all your mind.' [38]This is the first and greatest commandment. [39]And the second is like it: 'Love your neighbor as yourself.' [40]All the Law and the Prophets hang on these two commandments." NIV

_____

_____

_____

_____

_____

_____

_____

_____

_____

_____

_____

_____

_____

_____

_____

_____

_____

_____

_____

_____

_____

_____

Day 12   Date: _____

Luke 6:37-38

[37]"Stop judging others, and you will not be judged. Stop criticizing others, or it will all come back on you. If you forgive others, you will be forgiven. [38]If you give, you will receive. Your gift will return to you in full measure, pressed down, shaken together to make room for more, and running over. Whatever measure you use in giving--large or small--it will be used to measure what is given back to you." NLT

_____

_____

_____

_____

_____

_____

_____

_____

_____

_____

_____

_____

_____

_____

_____

_____

_____

_____

_____

_____

Date: _____

John 13:2-5, 12-17

²The evening meal was being served, and the devil had already prompted Judas Iscariot, son of Simon, to betray Jesus. ³Jesus knew that the Father had put all things under his power, and that he had come from God and was returning to God; ⁴so he got up from the meal, took off his outer clothing, and wrapped a towel around his waist. ⁵After that, he poured water into a basin and began to wash his disciples' feet, drying them with the towel that was wrapped around him.

¹²When he had finished washing their feet, he put on his clothes and returned to his place. "Do you understand what I have done for you?" he asked them. ¹³"You call me 'Teacher' and 'Lord,' and rightly so, for that is what I am. ¹⁴Now that I, your Lord and Teacher, have washed your feet, you also should wash one another's feet. ¹⁵I have set you an example that you should do as I have done for you. ¹⁶I tell you the truth, no servant is greater than his master, nor is a messenger greater than the one who sent him. ¹⁷Now that you know these things, you will be blessed if you do them. NIV

The wonderful thing that occurs during this entire process is that the more we give, the more we receive. The more captivated I am by my wife's love, the more she is captivated by mine. The more I focus on her, the more she focuses on me. The more I pour into the relationship, the more that is poured out to me. The more exhilarated I become over her love, the more exhilarated she becomes over mine. Can you imagine the kind of relationship that could exist if two people were so fanatically in love with each other that they were falling all over themselves trying to out love each other? We need more fanatics in our marriages. (UDM, page 74)

Day 14

Date: _____

John 13:34-35

[34]"Let me give you a new command: Love one another. In the same way I loved you, you love one another. [35]This is how everyone will recognize that you are my disciples--when they see the love you have for each other." MSG

_____

_____

_____

_____

_____

_____

_____

_____

_____

_____

_____

_____

_____

_____

_____

_____

_____

_____

_____

_____

_____

_____

_____

Day 15   Date: _____

Romans 12:8-10

[8]If your gift is to encourage others, do it! If you have money, share it generously. If God has given you leadership ability, take the responsibility seriously. And if you have a gift for showing kindness to others, do it gladly. [9]Don't just pretend that you love others. Really love them. Hate what is wrong. Stand on the side of the good. [10]Love each other with genuine affection, and take delight in honoring each other. NLT

_____

_____

_____

_____

_____

_____

_____

_____

_____

_____

_____

_____

_____

_____

_____

_____

_____

_____

_____

1 Corinthians 6:18-20

[18]There is a sense in which sexual sins are different from all others. In sexual sin we violate the sacredness of our own bodies, these bodies that were made for God-given and God-modeled love, for "becoming one" with another. [19]Or didn't you realize that your body is a sacred place, the place of the Holy Spirit? Don't you see that you can't live however you please, squandering what God paid such a high price for? The physical part of you is not some piece of property belonging to the spiritual part of you. [20]God owns the whole works. So let people see God in and through your body. MSG

Let's reduce it (emotional differences between men and women) to a useful oversimplification: men derive self-esteem by being respected; women feel worthy when they are loved. This may be the most important personality distinction between the sexes.

This understanding helps explain the unique views of marriage as seen by men and women. A man can be contented with a kind of business partnership in marriage, provided sexual privileges are part of the arrangement. As long as his wife prepares his dinner each evening, is reasonably amiable, and doesn't nag him during football season, he can be satisfied. The romantic element is nice—but not necessary. However, this kind of surface relationship drives his wife utterly wild with frustration. She must have something more meaningful. Women yearn to be the special sweethearts of their men, being respected and appreciated and loved with tenderness. This is why a housewife often thinks about her husband during the day and eagerly awaits his arrival home; it explains why their wedding anniversary is more important to her, and why he gets clobbered when he forgets it. It explains why she is constantly "reaching" for him when he is at home, trying to pull him out of the newspaper or television set; it explains why "Absence of Romantic Love in My Marriage" ranked so high as a source of depression among women, whereas men would have rated it somewhere in the vicinity of last place. (Dobson, 64-65)

Date: _____

1 Corinthians 7:1-7

[1]Now, getting down to the questions you asked in your letter to me. First, Is it a good thing to have sexual relations?
[2]Certainly—but only within a certain context. It's good for a man to have a wife, and for a woman to have a husband. Sexual drives are strong, but marriage is strong enough to contain them and provide for a balanced and fulfilling sexual life in a world of sexual disorder. [3]The marriage bed must be a place of mutuality—the husband seeking to satisfy his wife, the wife seeking to satisfy her husband. [4]Marriage is not a place to "stand up for your rights." Marriage is a decision to serve the other, whether in bed or out. [5]Abstaining from sex is permissible for a period of time if you both agree to it, and if it's for the purposes of prayer and fasting—but only for such times. Then come back together again. Satan has an ingenious way of tempting us when we least expect it. [6]I'm not, understand, commanding these periods of abstinence—only providing my best counsel if you should choose them.
[7]Sometimes I wish everyone were single like me—a simpler life in many ways! But celibacy is not for everyone any more than marriage is. God gives the gift of the single life to some, the gift of the married life to others. MSG

The adventure of loving our wives has begun. It is not her place to pursue us. The quest of pursuing our wives has been given to us by the King. The courtship of our wives is a life-long undertaking. The adventure is to rekindle the passion. The adventure is to grow old together and with deeper levels of intimacy. Let's grow more in love each day with our wives. Let's journey together to learn and understand the culture and language of women. (UDM, 113)

Date: _____

1 Corinthians 13:1-13

[1] If I could speak in any language in heaven or on earth but didn't love others, I would only be making meaningless noise like a loud gong or a clanging cymbal. [2] If I had the gift of prophecy, and if I knew all the mysteries of the future and knew everything about everything, but didn't love others, what good would I be? And if I had the gift of faith so that I could speak to a mountain and make it move, without love I would be no good to anybody. [3] If I gave everything I have to the poor and even sacrificed my body, I could boast about it; but if I didn't love others, I would be of no value whatsoever.

[4] Love is patient and kind. Love is not jealous or boastful or proud [5] or rude. Love does not demand its own way. Love is not irritable, and it keeps no record of when it has been wronged. [6] It is never glad about injustice but rejoices whenever the truth wins out. [7] Love never gives up, never loses faith, is always hopeful, and endures through every circumstance.

[8] Love will last forever, but prophecy and speaking in unknown languages and special knowledge will all disappear. [9] Now we know only a little, and even the gift of prophecy reveals little! [10] But when the end comes, these special gifts will all disappear.

[11] It's like this: When I was a child, I spoke and thought and reasoned as a child does. But when I grew up, I put away childish things. [12] Now we see things imperfectly as in a poor mirror, but then we will see everything with perfect clarity. All that I know now is partial and incomplete, but then I will know everything completely, just as God knows me now.

[13] There are three things that will endure—faith, hope, and love—and the greatest of these is love.   NLT

Being heard is so close to being loved that for the average person they are almost indistinguishable. To say something you value deeply to another and to have him or her value it equally by listening to it carefully and appreciatively is the most universal way of exchanging social interest and demonstrating affection. (Augsburger, 12)

2 Corinthians 5:17

[17] Therefore if anyone is in Christ, he is a new creature; the old things passed away; behold, new things have come. NASB

Philippians 4:13

[13] I can do all things through Him who strengthens me. NASB

_____

_____

_____

_____

_____

_____

_____

_____

_____

_____

_____

_____

_____

_____

_____

_____

_____

_____

_____

_____

_____

_____

Day 20

Date: _____

Ephesians 4:26-27

[26]When angry, do not sin; do not ever let your wrath (your exasperation, your fury or indignation) last until the sun goes down. [27]Leave no [such] room or foothold for the devil [give no opportunity to him].   AMP

_____

_____

_____

_____

_____

_____

_____

_____

_____

_____

_____

_____

_____

_____

_____

_____

_____

_____

_____

_____

_____

_____

_____

Ephesians 5:15-21

[15] Take care how you live. Do not live like people who are not wise, but live like people who are wise.

[16] Make good use of time because people live in very wrong ways these days.

[17] So then, be wise and understand what the Lord wants.

[18] Do not get drunk with wine. That is living in a wrong way. But be filled with the Spirit.

[19] Speak to one another by the songs in the holy writings, and songs of praise, and Christian songs. Sing and make a joyful noise in your hearts to the Lord.

[20] Always thank God the Father for all things in the name of our Lord Jesus Christ.

[21] Give way to each other because you respect Christ. WE

If you want your marriage to work, remember to always look for the beauty and not the spot. Whether it be a spouse, a child, a neighbor, a boss, or a friend, you can find as many spots as you want to look for. (Vannoy, 52)

A common myth in our society is that conflict is bad. But conflict can be a primary motivator and an indicator of change. Solving conflict doesn't have to be only a win-lose situation. (Vannoy, 52)

We could put up ten-foot banners around the house reminding our children (spouses) how much we love them or how special they are, and yet these will have far less impact than a simple act of truly listening. (Vannoy, 111)

Research shows that you have a greater impact on people by how you listen than by what you say. (Vannoy, 111)

Ephesians 5:22-24

[22]Wives, submit to your husbands as to the Lord. [23]For the husband is the head of the wife as Christ is the head of the church, his body, of which he is the Savior. [24]Now as the church submits to Christ, so also wives should submit to their husbands in everything.   NIV

_____

_____

_____

_____

_____

_____

_____

_____

_____

_____

_____

_____

_____

_____

_____

_____

_____

_____

_____

Day 23   Date: _____

Hebrews 3:12-13

[12]See to it, brothers, that none of you has a sinful, unbelieving heart that turns away from the living God. [13]But encourage one another daily, as long as it is called Today, so that none of you may be hardened by sin's deceitfulness.   NIV

_____

_____

_____

_____

_____

_____

_____

_____

_____

_____

_____

_____

_____

_____

_____

_____

_____

_____

_____

_____

Ephesians 5:25-33

[25]Husbands, go all out in your love for your wives, exactly as Christ did for the church—a love marked by giving, not getting. [26]Christ's love makes the church whole. His words evoke her beauty. Everything he does and says is designed to bring the best out of her, [27]dressing her in dazzling white silk, radiant with holiness. [28]And that is how husbands ought to love their wives. They're really doing themselves a favor—since they're already "one" in marriage.

[29]No one abuses his own body, does he? No, he feeds and pampers it. That's how Christ treats us, the church, [30]since we are part of his body. [31]And this is why a man leaves father and mother and cherishes his wife. No longer two, they become "one flesh." [32]This is a huge mystery, and I don't pretend to understand it all. What is clearest to me is the way Christ treats the church. [33]And this provides a good picture of how each husband is to treat his wife, loving himself in loving her, and how each wife is to honor her husband.   MSG

1 Peter 3:7

[7]   You husbands in the same way, live with your wives in an understanding way, as with someone weaker, since she is a woman; and show her honor as a fellow heir of the grace of life, so that your prayers will not be hindered.   NASB

"Before I got married, I had to make a decision. I knew that when I married Beattie, I was going to marry him, warts and all. My decision was not to get rid of the warts, but whether I was willing to live with him, warts and all."   (From my mother-in-law)

Philippians 2:3-4

[3]Do nothing from factional motives [through contentiousness, strife, self-ishness, or for unworthy ends] or prompted by conceit and empty arro-gance. Instead, in the true spirit of humility (lowliness of mind) let each regard the others as better than and superior to himself [thinking more highly of one another than you do of yourselves]. [4]Let each of you esteem and look upon and be concerned for not [merely] his own interests, but also each for the interests of others. AMP

Philippians 2:6-8

[6]Who, although being essentially one with God and in the form of God possessing the fullness of the attributes which make God God], did not think this equality with God was a thing to be eagerly grasped or retained, [7]But stripped Himself [of all privileges and   rightful dignity], so as to assume the guise of a servant (slave), in that He became like men and was born a human being. [8]And after He had appeared in human form, He abased and humbled Himself [still further] and carried His obedience to the extreme of death, even the death of the cross! AMP

Now I have not written this book to bad-rap American men. We've had plenty of that in recent years. It has become popular to depict father as an idiot, a bigot, an exploiter, a misogynist, a football fanatic, a sex-maniac, and a self-centered egotist. To hear some angry females tell it, men are lower than a snake on snowshoes. Being a man myself, I tend to take those charges rather personally. But it is true, I believe, that too many men do not understand the emotional needs of their wives. They live in a vastly different world with ample frustrations of their own. Either they are unable to put themselves in a woman's place, seeing and feeling what she experiences, or else they are preoccupied with their own work, and simply aren't listening. (Dobson, 13)

1 John 1:5-10

[5]Jesus told us that God is light and doesn't have any darkness in him. Now we are telling you. [6]If we say that we share in life with God and keep on living in the dark, we are lying and are not living by the truth. [7]But if we live in the light, as God does, we share in life with each other. And the blood of his Son Jesus washes all our sins away. [8]If we say that we have not sinned, we are fooling ourselves, and the truth isn't in our hearts. [9]But if we confess our sins to God, he can always be trusted to forgive us and take our sins away.

[10]If we say that we have not sinned, we make God a liar, and his message isn't in our hearts. CEV

"Remember who you are!"

"Simba, you are more than you have become!"

"It is time!"

(From *The Lion King*)

Day 27

Date: _____

James 1:19-20

[19]My dear friends, you should be quick to listen and slow to speak or to get angry. [20]If you are angry, you cannot do any of the good things that God wants done. CEV

_____

_____

_____

_____

_____

_____

_____

_____

_____

_____

_____

_____

_____

_____

_____

_____

_____

_____

_____

_____

_____

_____

Day 28

Date: _____

1 Peter 3:8-9

[8]Finally, all of you should agree and have concern and love for each other. You should also be kind and humble. [9]Don't be hateful and insult people just because they are hateful and insult you. Instead, treat everyone with kindness. You are God's chosen ones, and he will bless you.... CEV

James 5:16

[16] Therefore, confess your sins to one another, and pray for one another so that you may be healed. The effective prayer of a righteous man can accomplish much. NASB

James 5:16

[16]Make this your common practice: Confess your sins to each other and pray for each other so that you can live together whole and healed. The prayer of a person living right with God is something powerful to be reckoned with. MSG

James 5:16

[16]Confess to one another therefore your faults (your slips, your false steps, your offenses, your sins) and pray [also] for one another, that you may be healed and restored [to a spiritual tone of mind and heart]. The earnest (heartfelt, continued) prayer of a righteous man makes tremendous power available [dynamic in its working]. AMP

"Here, with us, 'tis different, for we're a family-like, and we've each other to share with. A family is a place where a body can share the no-account things, can talk of the little matters important only to ourselves, where we can laugh and cry and tell of the day-by-day happenings and then forget them...."

"You want to remember, Peg, just romance is not enough. You may often imagine yourself in love, but always remember you have to live with that person from day to day, in sickness and in health, as they say.

You will want to be proud of him when you introduce him to your friends, and you want him to be comfortable with them, as you must be with his friends. One must never marry a man thinking he will change or that you will change him. If he does or you do, then he will not be the same man you married, and the less for it."

                    (Louis L'Amour, *The Cherokee Trail*)

1 John 4:7-12

[7]Dear friends, let us love one another, for love comes from God. Everyone who loves has been born of God and knows God. [8]Whoever does not love does not know God, because God is love. [9]This is how God showed his love among us: He sent his one and only Son into the world that we might live through him. [10]This is love: not that we loved God, but that he loved us and sent his Son as an atoning sacrifice for our sins. [11]Dear friends, since God so loved us, we also ought to love one another. [12]No one has ever seen God; but if we love one another, God lives in us and his love is made complete in us.   NIV

Tell Her So

Amid the cares of married life,
In spite of toil and business strife,
If you value your sweet wife,
      Tell her so!

There was a time you thought it bliss
To get the favor of a kiss;
A dozen now won't come amiss—
      Tell her so!

Don't act as if she's passed her prime,
As though to please her were a crime—
If e'er you loved her, now's the time;
      Tell her so!

You are hers and hers alone;
Well you know she's all your own;
Don't wait to carve it on the stone—
      Tell her so!

Never let her heart grow cold;
Richer beauties will unfold.
She is worth her weight in gold;
      Tell her so!   (Peterson, author unknown, 69)

1 John 4:19-21

[19]We love because God loved us first. [20]But if we say we love God and don't love each other, we are liars. We cannot see God. So how can we love God, if we don't love the people we can see? [21]The commandment that God has given us is: "Love God and love each other!"   CEV

Words

I saw her drooping shoulders
Her sad, misty eyes
As his bitter words of sarcasm
Blew across her animation
And choked the story
She longed so much to share...

Words!
O dear God
Words can be so devastating
So destructive.
They shock and numb
They sting and torment.
In three brief minutes
They can disfigure a soul.
They permeate the air
Like suffocating poison.
Lord, Your own Word convicts us:
"So also the tongue is a small thing
But what enormous damage it can do."
Teach us to cope tactfully
Even in moments of disagreement.
Make us carefully selective
And lovingly protective
In the creative use of words.

(Calkin, 141)

References

Augsburger, David. *Caring Enough to Hear and Be Heard.* Ventura: Regal Books, 1982.

Calkin, Ruth Harms. *Marriage Is So Much More, Lord.* Wheaton: Living Books, 1986.

Dobson, Dr. James. *What Wives Wish Their Husbands Knew About Women.* Wheaton: Tyndale House, 1975.

Hendley, Jeff. *Upside Down Marriage.* Fairfax, Va: Xulon Press, 2002.

L'Amour, Louis. *The Cherokee Trail.* New York: Bantam Books, 1982.

Peck, M. Scott, MD. *The Road Less Traveled.* New York: Simon and Shuster, 1978.

Peterson, J. Allen, ed. *For Men Only.* Wheaton: Tyndale House, 1978.

Vannoy, Steven W. *The 10 Greatest Gifts I Give My Children.* New York: Simon and Shuster, 1994.

About the Author

For most of his life Jeff's brothers have accused him of being a full time student. Too many years in school, eleven years working in the family business, and a dozen years in various forms of ministry are the make up of his career. Jeff has served in management, as a Pastor to college students, as an Associate Pastor, as a Senior Pastor and as an Executive Director of a start-up program for abandoned and neglected children.

Today, he is the Director of Upside Down Ministries, Inc. Upside Down Ministries is a non-profit organization that seeks to build and develop healthy relationships through writing, speaking, mentoring and conducting workshops.

He and his wife Libbi have been actively involved with Young Life as volunteer leaders and serving on a Young Life Committee. Jeff and Libbi have been married over 26 years. They have five children: Kristy, Billy, Dickson, Todd and Bo. Home is in Boone, North Carolina.

Need a Speaker?

Click on **www.upsidedownministries.com**   for more information about having Jeff Hendley speak to your group or hold a conference or workshop.

Ordering Materials:

You can order materials through the website or contact Jeff Hendley...

Jeff Hendley
Upside Down Ministries, Inc.
PO Box 2567 • Boone, NC 28607
jeff@hendleys.net

Printed in the United States
29974LVS00001B/103-177